OSTEOAR
PLANT-BA{
COOKBOOK FOR
BEGINNERS

30 Easy Anti-Inflammatory Vegan Recipes for Pain Relief and Healthy Living

WALLACE BURKE

GAIN ACCESS TO MORE BOOKS FROM ME

TABLE OF CONTENT

INTRODUCTION

Elara, an elderly woman, resided in a lovely town surrounded by lush greenery. Her once-nimble fingers had become twisted by the inexorable grip of osteoarthritis, making each day a symphony of pains and creaks. The vivid tapestry of her garden, once lovingly nurtured, had begun to wither, matching the agony in her joints.

Elara's life was a tribute to perseverance, but the unrelenting anguish had begun to weaken her unbreakable spirit. She had tried every treatment the local physicians could suggest, from poultices to potions, but comfort remained as elusive as a shadow at midday.

One day, a wandering herbalist visited the community. He was an ancient friend of the land, with knowledge as broad as the forests he frequented. He recognized Elara's struggle and, with a sweet grin, suggested a less-traveled path—a plant-based diet that may relieve her inflamed joints and revitalize her tired bones.

Elara, skeptical but desperate, decided to go on this environmentally conscious path. She developed her garden into a refuge of medicinal herbs and veggies with the help of an herbalist. Turmeric, with its golden color, promised anti-inflammatory benefits. Ginger offered its fiery touch, fanning the flames of healing. Leafy greens, which are high in antioxidants, painted her dishes in vibrant colors.

Elara's diet altered along with the seasons. She learned to listen to the earth's messages, selecting meals that flourished in accordance with her body's needs. Her kitchen became her pharmacy, where she created foods that were spiritually beneficial.

With each passing day, the tightness in her joints subsided. The anguish that had previously shouted in her ears had now become a whisper. Her fingers, previously imprisoned in misery, rediscover their dance among the flowers and leaves of her garden.

The news of Elara's metamorphosis traveled around the community like a cool wind. Her home became a haven for those in need, and her garden was a tribute to nature's healing power.

Elara, in her final years, had discovered a truth that she imparted to anybody who would listen: Nature, in its infinite wisdom, offers the secret to healing. And in her heart, a seed of thankfulness sprouted for the sorrow that had led her to the earth's healing embrace.

DELICIOUS OSTEOARTHRITIS PLANT BASED RECIPES

1. *Turmeric-Ginger Stir-Fry*

Ingredients:

1 cup of quinoa (uncooked)

2 tablespoons olive oil

1 small onion, finely chopped

2 cloves garlic, minced

1 tablespoon fresh ginger, grated

1 tablespoon turmeric powder

1 cup broccoli florets

1 cup sliced bell peppers (mix of red, yellow, and green)

1 cup carrot, julienned

1 cup spinach leaves

1/4 cup unsalted cashews

2 tablespoons low-sodium soy sauce or tamari

Salt and pepper to taste

Preparation Method:

Cook quinoa according to package instructions; set aside.

Heat olive oil in a large skillet over medium heat. Add onion, garlic, and ginger, sautéing until onion is translucent.

Stir in turmeric powder, mixing well to combine.

Add broccoli, bell peppers, and carrots to the skillet, sautéing for 5-7 minutes until vegetables are tender but still crisp.

Toss in spinach leaves, allowing them to wilt.

Stir in cooked quinoa, cashews, and soy sauce, mixing well. Season with salt and pepper to taste.

Cook for an additional 2-3 minutes, ensuring everything is heated through and well combined.

Nutritional Value (per serving):

Calories: 320 kcal

Protein: 10g

Fiber: 6g

Fat: 15g (Saturated: 2g, Unsaturated: 11g)

Cooking Time: 30 minutes

2. Anti-Inflammatory Sweet Potato and Kale Soup

Ingredients:

1 tablespoon coconut oil

1 large onion, diced

2 cloves garlic, minced

1 tablespoon grated fresh ginger

2 large sweet potatoes, peeled and cubed

4 cups vegetable broth

1 teaspoon turmeric powder

1/2 teaspoon cayenne pepper (optional)

4 cups kale, de-stemmed and chopped

1 can (14 oz) coconut milk

Salt and pepper to taste

Pumpkin seeds for garnish

Preparation Method:

In a large pot, heat coconut oil over medium heat. Add onion and garlic, sautéing until the onion is soft.

Stir in ginger, sweet potatoes, turmeric, and cayenne pepper, cooking for about 2 minutes until fragrant.

Add vegetable broth and bring to a boil. Reduce heat to simmer and cover, cooking until sweet potatoes are tender, about 20 minutes.

Add kale and coconut milk, stirring until the kale is wilted and the soup is heated through.

Use an immersion blender to partially blend the soup, leaving some chunks for texture, or blend about half the soup in a blender and mix back in for a creamy yet chunky texture.

Season with salt and pepper to taste. Serve hot, garnished with pumpkin seeds.

Nutritional Value (per serving):

Calories: 260 kcal

Protein: 5g

Fiber: 5g

Fat: 14g (Saturated: 12g, Unsaturated: 2g)

Cooking Time: 40 minutes

3. Anti-Inflammatory Turmeric Lentil Soup

Ingredients:

1 cup red lentils, rinsed

1 large carrot, diced (about 1/2 cup)

1 stalk celery, diced (about 1/2 cup)

1 small onion, finely chopped (about 1 cup)

2 cloves garlic, minced

1 teaspoon turmeric powder

1/2 teaspoon ground ginger

1/4 teaspoon black pepper

1 tablespoon olive oil

4 cups low-sodium vegetable broth

1 cup water

2 cups baby spinach leaves

Salt to taste

Lemon wedges for serving

Preparation Method:

In a large pot, heat olive oil over medium heat. Add the onion, carrot, and celery. Sauté for 5 minutes until the vegetables soften.

Add minced garlic, turmeric, ginger, and black pepper. Cook for another minute until fragrant.

Pour in the rinsed lentils, vegetable broth, and water. Stir well to combine all the ingredients.

Bring to a boil, then reduce the heat to low, cover, and simmer for 20-25 minutes, or until lentils are soft.

Stir in the spinach leaves and continue to simmer until the spinach wilts, about 2-3 minutes.

Taste and adjust seasoning with salt as needed.

Serve hot with a squeeze of lemon juice for an extra flavor boost.

Nutritional Value (per serving):

Calories: 210

Protein: 12g

Fiber: 10g

Fat: 4g

Cooking Time: 35-40 minutes

4. Omega-3 Rich Chia and Flaxseed Pudding

Ingredients:

3 tablespoons chia seeds

1 tablespoon ground flaxseed

1 cup unsweetened almond milk (or any plant-based milk of your choice)

1/2 teaspoon vanilla extract

1 tablespoon maple syrup or agave nectar (optional for sweetness)

Fresh berries (strawberries, blueberries, raspberries) for topping

A pinch of cinnamon (optional)

Preparation Method:

In a mixing bowl, combine the chia seeds, ground flaxseed, almond milk, vanilla extract, and maple syrup. Whisk until well combined.

Let the mixture sit for about 5 minutes, then stir again to break up any clumps of chia seeds.

Cover the bowl and refrigerate for at least 2 hours, or overnight, until it has a pudding-like consistency.

When ready to serve, give the pudding a good stir. If it's too thick, you can thin it with a little more almond milk.

Spoon the pudding into serving bowls and top with fresh berries and a sprinkle of cinnamon if desired.

Nutritional Value (per serving):

Calories: 180

Protein: 5g

Fiber: 9g

Omega-3 Fatty Acids: 4g

Cooking Time: 5 minutes (plus at least 2 hours for setting in the refrigerator)

5. Anti-Inflammatory Turmeric and Ginger Tea

Ingredients:

2 cups of water

1-inch fresh turmeric root, grated (about 1 tablespoon)

1-inch fresh ginger root, grated (about 1 tablespoon)

1 tablespoon lemon juice

1 teaspoon raw honey (optional, for sweetness)

A pinch of black pepper (to enhance turmeric absorption)

Preparation Method:

In a small saucepan, bring the water to a boil.

Add the grated turmeric and ginger to the boiling water and reduce the heat to simmer for about 10 minutes. This allows the flavors and beneficial compounds to infuse into the water.

Remove from heat and strain the tea into a cup to remove the turmeric and ginger pieces.

Stir in the lemon juice, and if desired, add honey for sweetness. Sprinkle a pinch of black pepper into the tea and stir well.

Enjoy your tea warm.

Nutritional Value (per serving):

Calories: 10 kcal

Carbohydrates: 2g

Dietary Fiber: 0.5g

Cooking Time: 15 minutes

6. Spinach and Berry Smoothie

Ingredients:

1 cup fresh spinach leaves

1/2 cup frozen mixed berries (such as blueberries, strawberries, and raspberries)

1 banana, peeled

1 tablespoon chia seeds

1 cup unsweetened almond milk (or plant-based milk of your choice)

1/2 teaspoon vanilla extract (optional for flavor)

Preparation Method:

Add the spinach, frozen berries, banana, chia seeds, and almond milk to a blender.

Blend on high speed until smooth and creamy. If the smoothie is too thick, you can add more almond milk to reach your desired consistency.

Pour the smoothie into a glass, and if you like, stir in the vanilla extract for an extra flavor boost.

Serve immediately for the freshest taste and the most nutrients.

Nutritional Value (per serving):

Calories: 200 kcal

Carbohydrates: 35g

Dietary Fiber: 8g

Protein: 5g

Cooking Time: 5 minutes

7. Quinoa and Roasted Vegetable Salad

Ingredients:

1 cup quinoa, uncooked

2 cups water

1 small sweet potato, peeled and diced

1 red bell pepper, chopped

1 zucchini, sliced into half-moons

2 tablespoons olive oil

1 teaspoon ground cumin

1/2 teaspoon paprika

Salt and pepper, to taste

1/4 cup chopped fresh parsley

Juice of 1 lemon

Preparation Method:

Preheat your oven to 400°F (200°C). Line a baking sheet with parchment paper.

Toss the sweet potato, red bell pepper, and zucchini with olive oil, cumin, paprika, salt, and pepper. Spread the vegetables on the prepared baking sheet in a single layer.

Roast the vegetables in the preheated oven for about 25-30 minutes, or until tender and slightly caramelized, stirring halfway through the cooking time.

While the vegetables are roasting, rinse the quinoa under cold water. In a medium saucepan, bring 2 cups of water to a boil. Add the quinoa, reduce the heat to low, cover, and simmer for about 15 minutes, or until the water is absorbed. Remove from heat and let it sit covered for 5 minutes. Fluff with a fork.

In a large bowl, combine the cooked quinoa and roasted vegetables. Add the chopped parsley and lemon juice, and toss everything together.

Season with additional salt and pepper if needed, and serve either warm or at room temperature.

Nutritional Value (per serving):

Calories: 260 kcal

Carbohydrates: 40g

Dietary Fiber: 6g

Protein: 8g

Cooking Time: 45 minutes

8. Turmeric-Ginger Tofu Stir-Fry

Ingredients:

200g firm tofu, cubed

1 tablespoon of olive oil

1 teaspoon of turmeric

1 teaspoon grated fresh ginger

2 garlic cloves, minced

1 cup of broccoli florets

1/2 cup sliced carrots

1/2 cup bell pepper strips

2 tablespoons low-sodium soy sauce

1 tablespoon sesame seeds

Salt and pepper to taste

Preparation Method:

Press the tofu to remove excess water and cut it into cubes.

Heat olive oil in a large pan over medium heat. Add turmeric, ginger, and garlic, sautéing for 1-2 minutes until fragrant.

Increase heat to medium-high, add tofu cubes, and stir-fry until golden, about 5-7 minutes.

Add broccoli, carrots, and bell peppers to the pan, stir-frying for another 5 minutes until vegetables are tender-crisp.

Pour soy sauce over the mixture, season with salt and pepper, and sprinkle with sesame seeds. Stir well to combine.

Serve hot.

Nutritional Value (per serving):

Calories: 250

Protein: 15g

Fiber: 4g

Fat: 15g

Cooking Time: 20 minutes

9. Quinoa and Black Bean Salad

Ingredients:

1 cup of quinoa

2 cups of water

1 can (15 oz) black beans, rinsed and drained

1 cup cherry tomatoes, halved

1 avocado, diced

1/2 red onion, finely chopped

1/4 cup chopped fresh cilantro

Juice of 1 lime

2 tablespoons extra-virgin olive oil

Salt and pepper to taste

Preparation Method:

Rinse quinoa under cold water. In a medium saucepan, bring 2 cups of water to a boil. Add quinoa, reduce heat to low, cover, and simmer for 15 minutes or until water is absorbed. Remove from heat and let sit, covered, for 5 minutes. Fluff with a fork.

In a large bowl, combine cooked quinoa, black beans, cherry tomatoes, avocado, red onion, and cilantro.

In a small bowl, whisk together the lime juice, olive oil, salt, and pepper. Pour over the quinoa mixture and toss to combine.

Serve chilled or at room temperature.

Nutritional Value (per serving):

Calories: 310

Protein: 10g

Fiber: 8g

Fat: 13g

Cooking Time: 25 minutes

10. Spinach and Walnut Pesto Pasta

Ingredients:

2 cups of fresh spinach leaves

1/2 cup walnuts

2 garlic cloves

1/2 cup nutritional yeast

1/4 cup extra-virgin olive oil

Juice of 1 lemon

Salt and pepper to taste

200g whole wheat pasta

Preparation Method:

Cook pasta according to package instructions until al dente. Drain and set aside.

In a food processor, blend spinach, walnuts, garlic, and nutritional yeast until finely chopped.

With the processor running, slowly add olive oil and lemon juice until the mixture becomes smooth. Season with salt and pepper.

Toss the pesto with the cooked pasta until evenly coated.

Serve immediately, garnished with additional walnuts if desired.

Nutritional Value (per serving):

Calories: 400

Protein: 15g

Fiber: 6g

Fat: 20g

Cooking Time: 20 minutes

11. Chickpea and Avocado Salad

Ingredients:

1 can (15 oz) chickpeas, rinsed and drained

1 ripe avocado, diced

1 large tomato, diced (about 1 cup)

1/2 cucumber, diced (about 1/2 cup)

1/4 cup red onion, finely chopped

2 tablespoons of fresh lemon juice (about 1 lemon)

2 tablespoons extra-virgin olive oil

1/4 teaspoon ground cumin

Salt and pepper to taste

1/4 cup fresh cilantro, chopped

Preparation Method:

In a large bowl, combine the chickpeas, avocado, tomato, cucumber, and red onion.

In a small bowl, whisk together the lemon juice, olive oil, ground cumin, salt, and pepper. Pour this dressing over the salad ingredients.

Gently toss the salad to ensure all ingredients are well coated with the dressing.

Sprinkle chopped cilantro over the salad just before serving.

Nutritional Value (per serving):

Calories: 290 kcal

Protein: 7g

Fiber: 9g

Fat: 15g

Cooking Time: 15 minutes

12. Broccoli and Almond Stir-Fry

Ingredients:

1 tablespoon sesame oil

4 cups of broccoli florets

1 red bell pepper, thinly sliced (about 1 cup)

2 tablespoons low-sodium soy sauce

1 tablespoon of rice vinegar

1 tablespoon of maple syrup

1/2 cup raw almonds, roughly chopped

2 cloves garlic, minced

1 teaspoon grated ginger

Sesame seeds for garnish (optional)

Cooked brown rice or quinoa for serving

Preparation Method:

In a small bowl, whisk together soy sauce, rice vinegar, and maple syrup. Set aside.

Heat sesame oil in a large pan or wok over medium-high heat. Add broccoli and bell pepper, stir-frying for about 5 minutes, until vegetables are just tender but still crisp.

Add garlic and ginger to the pan, cooking for another minute until fragrant. Pour the stir-fry sauce over the vegetables and toss to coat evenly.

Stir in the chopped almonds and cook for another 2-3 minutes, allowing the flavors to meld together.

Sprinkle with sesame seeds if desired, and serve hot over a bed of brown rice or quinoa.

Nutritional Value (per serving, excluding rice and quinoa):

Calories: 220 kcal

Protein: 7g

Fiber: 6g

Fat: 15g

Cooking Time: 20 minutes

13. Zucchini Noodle Salad with Peanut Dressing

Ingredients:

2 large zucchinis, spiralized into noodles

1 red bell pepper, thinly sliced

1 carrot, julienned

1/4 cup cilantro, chopped

1/4 cup green onions, chopped

1/4 cup peanuts, crushed for garnish

For the Peanut Dressing:

2 tablespoons of peanut butter

1 tablespoon soy sauce (or tamari for gluten-free)

1 tablespoon of lime juice

1 teaspoon maple syrup

1 clove garlic, minced

1/2 inch ginger, grated

Water to thin as needed

Preparation Method:

Combine the spiralized zucchini, sliced bell pepper, julienned carrot, cilantro, and green onions in a large bowl.

In a small bowl, whisk together peanut butter, soy sauce, lime juice, maple syrup, minced garlic, and grated ginger. Add water as needed to reach the desired consistency.

Pour the peanut dressing over the vegetable mixture and toss until well coated.

Garnish with crushed peanuts just before serving.

Nutritional Value (per serving):

Calories: 150 kcal

Protein: 6g

Fiber: 3g

Fat: 9g

Cooking Time: 15 minutes

14. Chickpea Stuffed Bell Peppers

Ingredients:

4 large bell peppers, halved and seeds removed

1 can (15 oz) chickpeas, rinsed and drained

1 cup quinoa, cooked

1/2 cup tomato sauce

1 zucchini, diced

1/2 cup of corn kernels

1 teaspoon of cumin

1 teaspoon smoked paprika

2 tablespoons of olive oil

Salt and pepper to taste

Fresh parsley for garnish

Preparation Method:

Preheat your oven to 375°F (190°C).

In a bowl, mix the chickpeas, cooked quinoa, tomato sauce, diced zucchini, corn, cumin, smoked paprika, salt, and pepper.

Brush the inside of each bell pepper half with olive oil and fill with the chickpea-quinoa mixture.

Place the stuffed peppers in a baking dish and cover with foil. Bake in the preheated oven for about 30 minutes, until the peppers are tender.

Garnish with fresh parsley before serving.

Nutritional Value (per serving):

Calories: 250 kcal

Protein: 8g

Fiber: 7g

Fat: 7g

Cooking Time: 45 minutes

15. Avocado and Bean Wrap

Ingredients:

2 whole-grain tortillas

1 ripe avocado, mashed

1 can (15 oz) black beans, rinsed and drained

1/2 cup cherry tomatoes, halved

1/4 cup red onion, finely chopped

2 tablespoons cilantro, chopped

Juice of 1 lime

Salt and pepper to taste

Leafy greens of choice (spinach, lettuce, etc.)

Preparation Method:

In a bowl, mix the mashed avocado, black beans, cherry tomatoes, red onion, cilantro, lime juice, salt, and pepper.

Lay out the tortillas and spread the avocado-bean mixture down the center of each. Top it with a handful of leafy greens.

Roll up the tortillas tightly, cut in half, and serve immediately.

Nutritional Value (per serving):

Calories: 320 kcal

Protein: 10g

Fiber: 12g

Fat: 15g

Cooking Time: 15 minutes

16. *Spiced Carrot Soup*

Ingredients:

1 tablespoon of olive oil

1 large onion, chopped (about 1 cup)

2 cloves garlic, minced

1 pound of peeled and diced carrots (about 4 cups)

4 cups of vegetable broth

1 teaspoon ground ginger

1 teaspoon of ground turmeric

Salt and pepper to taste

Pumpkin seeds for garnish

Preparation Method:

In a large pot, heat the olive oil over medium heat. Add the onion and garlic, and sauté until translucent.

Add the diced carrots to the pot and cook for a few minutes until they start to soften.

Pour in the vegetable broth, and add the ginger and turmeric. Season with salt and pepper.

Bring to a boil, then reduce heat and simmer for about 20 minutes or until the carrots are very soft.

Use an immersion blender to purée the soup until smooth. Adjust the seasoning as needed.

Serve hot, garnished with pumpkin seeds.

Nutritional Value (per serving):

Calories: 120 kcal

Protein: 2g

Fiber: 4g

Fat: 4g

Cooking Time: 30 minutes

17. Beet and Orange Salad

Ingredients:

3 medium beets, roasted, peeled, and sliced

2 oranges, peeled and sectioned

1/4 cup walnuts, toasted and chopped

2 cups mixed salad greens

For the dressing:

2 tablespoons of balsamic vinegar

1 tablespoon of olive oil

1 teaspoon Dijon mustard

Salt and pepper to taste

Preparation Method:

Arrange the salad greens on a plate. Top with sliced beets and orange sections.

In a small bowl, whisk together the balsamic vinegar, olive oil, and Dijon mustard. Season with salt and pepper.

Drizzle the dressing over the salad and sprinkle with toasted walnuts.

Nutritional Value (per serving):

Calories: 180 kcal

Protein: 4g

Fiber: 6g

Fat: 10g

Cooking Time: 15 minutes (excluding beet roasting time)

18. Cauliflower Steak with Walnut Pesto

Ingredients:

4 large cauliflower slices (steaks), about 1 inch thick

2 tablespoons of olive oil

Salt and pepper to taste

For the walnut pesto:

1/2 cup walnuts

1 cup of fresh basil leaves

2 cloves of garlic

1/4 cup nutritional yeast

1/4 cup olive oil

Salt to taste

Water, as needed for consistency

Preparation Method:

Preheat your oven to 400°F (200°C).

Place the cauliflower steaks on a baking sheet. Brush both sides with olive oil, and season with salt and pepper. Roast in the preheated oven for about 20 minutes, flipping halfway through, until tender and golden.

While the cauliflower is roasting, combine walnuts, basil, garlic, and nutritional yeast in a food processor. Pulse while drizzling in olive oil until a pesto consistency is reached. Add a little water if the pesto is too thick. Season with salt to taste.

Top each cauliflower steak with a generous dollop of walnut pesto before serving.

Nutritional Value (per serving):

Calories: 320 kcal

Protein: 8g

Fiber: 6g

Fat: 28g

Cooking Time: 30 minutes

19. Spinach and Mushroom Quinoa

Ingredients:

1 cup quinoa, rinsed

2 cups of vegetable broth

2 tablespoons of olive oil

1 onion, diced

2 cloves garlic, minced

2 cups mushrooms, sliced

3 cups of spinach leaves

Salt and pepper to taste

Lemon juice for serving

Preparation Method:

In a saucepan, combine quinoa and vegetable broth. Bring to a boil, reduce heat to low, cover, and simmer for 15 minutes or until the liquid is absorbed. Remove from heat and let sit covered for 5 minutes.

While the quinoa is cooking, heat olive oil in a skillet over medium heat. Add onion and garlic, sautéing until translucent. Add mushrooms and cook until they release their moisture and start to brown. Stir in the spinach and cook until just wilted. Season with salt and pepper.

Mix the cooked quinoa into the skillet with the vegetables. Adjust seasoning as needed.

Drizzle with lemon juice before serving.

Nutritional Value (per serving):

Calories: 260 kcal

Protein: 9g

Fiber: 5g

Fat: 10g

Cooking Time: 30 minutes

20. Stuffed Acorn Squash

Ingredients:

2 acorn squashes, halved and seeds removed

1 tablespoon of olive oil

Salt and pepper to taste

1 cup quinoa, cooked

1 can (15 oz) black beans, rinsed and drained

1/2 cup cranberries

1/2 cup pecans, chopped

1 teaspoon ground cinnamon

1/2 teaspoon ground nutmeg

Preparation Method:

Preheat the oven to 375°F (190°C). Brush the cut sides of the acorn squash with olive oil and season with salt and pepper. Place cut-side down on a baking sheet and roast until tender, about 25–30 minutes.

In a large bowl, combine cooked quinoa, black beans, cranberries, pecans, cinnamon, and nutmeg. Mix well.

Once the squash is roasted, fill each half with the quinoa mixture.

Return the stuffed squashes to the oven and bake for an additional 10 minutes.

Nutritional Value (per serving):

Calories: 350 kcal

Protein: 9g

Fiber: 8g

Fat: 13g

Cooking Time: 45 minutes

21. Cauliflower and Spinach Curry

Ingredients:

1 large cauliflower, cut into florets (about 4 cups)

3 cups fresh spinach, washed and chopped

1 large onion, finely chopped (about 1 cup)

2 cloves garlic, minced

1 inch of fresh ginger, grated (about 1 tablespoon)

1 can (14 oz) of coconut milk

1 tablespoon curry powder

1 teaspoon of turmeric

1/2 teaspoon cumin

2 tablespoons of olive oil

Salt and pepper to taste

Fresh cilantro for garnish

Preparation Method:

In a large skillet or wok, heat the olive oil over medium heat. Add the onion, garlic, and ginger, sautéing until the onion is translucent.

Stir in the curry powder, turmeric, and cumin, cooking for another minute until fragrant.

Add the cauliflower florets to the skillet, mixing well to coat with the spices. Cook for about 5 minutes.

Pour in the coconut milk, bring to a gentle simmer, cover, and cook for 15 minutes or until the cauliflower is tender.

Stir in the chopped spinach and cook until wilted, about 2–3 minutes. Season with salt and pepper.

Garnish with fresh cilantro before serving. Enjoy it with a side of brown rice or quinoa.

Nutritional Value (per serving):

Calories: 250 kcal

Protein: 5g

Fiber: 6g

Fat: 20g

Cooking Time: 30 minutes

22. Stuffed Acorn Squash with Quinoa and Cranberries

Ingredients:

2 acorn squashes, halved and seeds removed

1 cup quinoa, rinsed

2 cups of vegetable broth

1/2 cup dried cranberries

1/2 cup pecans, chopped

2 tablespoons of olive oil

1 teaspoon cinnamon

1/2 teaspoon nutmeg

Salt and pepper to taste

Parsley for garnish

Preparation Method:

Preheat the oven to 375°F (190°C). Brush the cut sides of the acorn squash with olive oil and season with salt and pepper. Place on a baking sheet, cut side down, and roast until tender, about 25–30 minutes.

In a saucepan, bring the vegetable broth to a boil. Add the quinoa, reduce the heat to low, cover, and simmer for 15 minutes or until all the liquid is absorbed. Let it sit covered for 5 minutes, then fluff it with a fork.

In a large bowl, mix the cooked quinoa, dried cranberries, pecans, cinnamon, and nutmeg.

Fill the roasted acorn squash halves with the quinoa mixture. Return to the oven and bake for another 10 minutes.

Garnish with parsley before serving.

Nutritional Value (per serving):

Calories: 400 kcal

Protein: 8g

Fiber: 8g

Fat: 18g

Cooking Time: 45 minutes

23. Beetroot and Carrot Salad with Orange Dressing

Ingredients:

3 medium beetroots, peeled and grated

3 large carrots, peeled and grated

1/4 cup walnuts, chopped

1/4 cup fresh parsley, chopped

For the orange dressing:

Juice of 2 oranges

2 tablespoons of olive oil

1 tablespoon apple cider vinegar

1 teaspoon of maple syrup

Salt and pepper to taste

Preparation Method:

In a large bowl, combine the grated beetroots, carrots, chopped walnuts, and parsley.

In a small bowl, whisk together the orange juice, olive oil, apple cider vinegar, maple syrup, salt, and pepper until well combined.

Pour the dressing over the salad and toss well to ensure everything is evenly coated.

Let the salad sit for about 10 minutes before serving to allow the flavors to meld.

Nutritional Value (per serving):

Calories: 220 kcal

Protein: 4g

Fiber: 6g

Fat: 14g

Cooking Time: 20 minutes

24. Roasted Sweet Potato and Chickpea Salad

Ingredients:

2 large sweet potatoes, peeled and cubed (about 4 cups)

1 can (15 oz) chickpeas, drained and rinsed

1 tablespoon of olive oil

1 teaspoon smoked paprika

1/2 teaspoon garlic powder

1/4 teaspoon cayenne pepper (optional)

Salt and pepper to taste

4 cups of mixed salad greens

1/4 cup tahini

Juice of 1 lemon

2 tablespoons of water (to thin the dressing)

2 tablespoons of pumpkin seeds

Preparation Method:

Preheat the oven to 400°F (200°C). Toss the sweet potatoes and chickpeas with olive oil, smoked paprika, garlic powder, cayenne pepper, salt, and pepper. Spread on a baking sheet and roast for 25–30 minutes, stirring halfway through, until the sweet potatoes are tender.

Whisk together tahini, lemon juice, and water until smooth. Adjust the consistency with more water if needed, and season with salt to taste.

Toss the roasted sweet potato and chickpea mixture with the mixed greens. Drizzle with tahini dressing and sprinkle with pumpkin seeds.

Serve immediately or keep the components separate until ready to serve.

Nutritional Value (per serving):

Calories: 300 kcal

Protein: 9g

Fiber: 8g

Fat: 14g

Cooking Time: 40 minutes

25. Spiced Lentil Soup

Ingredients:

1 cup red lentils, rinsed

4 cups of vegetable broth

1 can (14 oz) diced tomatoes

1 medium onion, diced (about 1 cup)

2 carrots, peeled and diced (about 1 cup)

2 cloves garlic, minced

1 teaspoon of ground turmeric

1 teaspoon ground cumin

1/2 teaspoon ground ginger

1/2 teaspoon paprika

2 tablespoons of olive oil

Salt and pepper to taste

2 cups of spinach leaves

Lemon wedges for serving

Preparation Method:

In a large pot, heat the olive oil over medium heat. Add the onions and carrots, sautéing until they start to soften, about 5 minutes. Add the garlic and cook for another minute.

Stir in the lentils, diced tomatoes, turmeric, cumin, ginger, and paprika. Cook for a couple of minutes, allowing the spices to become fragrant.

Pour in the vegetable broth, bring to a boil, then reduce the heat and simmer, covered, for about 20 minutes or until the lentils are tender.

Add the spinach and cook until wilted. Season with salt and pepper, to taste.

Serve the soup hot with lemon wedges on the side.

Nutritional Value (per serving):

Calories: 250 kcal

Protein: 12g

Fiber: 10g

Fat: 5g

Cooking Time: 35 minutes

26. Quinoa and Vegetable Stuffed Bell Peppers

Ingredients:

4 large bell peppers, halved and seeds removed

1 cup quinoa, rinsed

2 cups of vegetable broth

1 can (15 oz) black beans, drained and rinsed

1 cup of corn kernels (fresh or frozen)

1 cup cherry tomatoes, diced

1 cup spinach, chopped

1 teaspoon of cumin

1 teaspoon paprika

1 teaspoon garlic powder

Salt and pepper to taste

2 tablespoons of olive oil

Preparation Method:

Preheat the oven to 375°F (190°C).

In a medium-sized saucepan, bring the vegetable broth to a boil. Add the quinoa, reduce heat to low, cover, and simmer for 15-20 minutes or until the quinoa is cooked and the liquid is absorbed.

In a large mixing bowl, combine the cooked quinoa, black beans, corn, cherry tomatoes, spinach, cumin, paprika, garlic powder, salt, and pepper. Mix well.

Place the bell pepper halves in a baking dish. Stuff each pepper with the quinoa and vegetable mixture.

Drizzle olive oil over the stuffed peppers.

Bake in the preheated oven for 25–30 minutes, or until the peppers are tender.

Serve the stuffed peppers warm. Enjoy your delicious and nutritious plant-based meal!

Nutritional Value (per serving):

Calories: 320

Protein: 12g

Carbohydrates: 56g

Fiber: 11g

Fat: 7g

Saturated Fat: 1g

Sodium: 580mg

Cooking Time: 50–60 minutes

27. Lentil and Vegetable Curry

Ingredients:

1 cup dried green lentils, rinsed

4 cups of vegetable broth

1 tablespoon of coconut oil

1 onion, finely chopped

3 cloves garlic, minced

1 tablespoon ginger, grated

1 tablespoon curry powder

1 teaspoon of turmeric

1 teaspoon of cumin

1 teaspoon of coriander

1 can (14 oz) diced tomatoes

1 can (14 oz) of coconut milk

2 cups mixed vegetables (e.g., carrots, bell peppers, broccoli), chopped

Salt and pepper to taste

Fresh cilantro for garnish

Preparation Method:

In a large pot, combine the lentils and vegetable broth. Bring to a boil, then reduce heat to low, cover, and simmer for 20–25 minutes or until lentils are tender.

In a separate skillet, heat coconut oil over medium heat. Add chopped onion, garlic, and ginger. Sauté until the onion is translucent.

Add curry powder, turmeric, cumin, and coriander to the skillet. Stir well to coat the onions with the spices.

Add the diced tomatoes (with their juice) and coconut milk to the skillet. Bring to a simmer.

Transfer the lentils to the skillet and mix well. Add the chopped vegetables. Season with salt and pepper.

Simmer for an additional 15-20 minutes or until the vegetables are tender.

Garnish with fresh cilantro before serving.

Nutritional Value (per serving):

Calories: 420

Protein: 18g

Carbohydrates: 50g

Fiber: 15g

Fat: 18g

Saturated Fat: 14g

Sodium: 700mg

28. Sweet Potato and Black Bean Chili

Ingredients:

2 large sweet potatoes, peeled and diced

1 can (15 oz) black beans, drained and rinsed

1 can (14 oz) diced tomatoes

1 onion, diced

3 cloves garlic, minced

1 bell pepper, diced

1 cup of corn kernels (fresh or frozen)

1 tablespoon chili powder

1 teaspoon of cumin

1 teaspoon smoked paprika

1/2 teaspoon cinnamon

4 cups of vegetable broth

Salt and pepper to taste

2 tablespoons of olive oil

Avocado slices for garnish (optional)

Preparation Method:

In a large pot, heat olive oil over medium heat. Add diced onion, garlic, and bell pepper. Sauté until the vegetables are softened.

Add sweet potatoes, black beans, diced tomatoes, corn, chili powder, cumin, smoked paprika, and cinnamon to the pot. Stir well to combine.

Pour in the vegetable broth and bring the chili to a boil. Reduce heat to low, cover, and simmer for 20–25 minutes or until the sweet potatoes are tender.

Season with salt and pepper, to taste.

Serve the chili in bowls, garnishing with avocado slices if desired.

Nutritional Value (per serving):

Calories: 380

Protein: 12g

Carbohydrates: 70g

Fiber: 15g

Fat: 8g

Saturated Fat: 1g

Sodium: 820mg

Cooking Time: 30-35 minutes

29. Spinach and Chickpea Salad with Lemon-Tahini Dressing

Ingredients:

4 cups of fresh spinach leaves

1 can (15 oz) chickpeas, drained and rinsed

1 cup cherry tomatoes, halved

1 cucumber, diced

1/4 cup red onion, thinly sliced

1/4 cup fresh parsley, chopped

1/4 cup tahini

3 tablespoons of lemon juice

2 tablespoons of water

1 tablespoon of olive oil

1 clove garlic, minced

Salt and pepper to taste

Preparation Method:

In a large salad bowl, combine spinach, chickpeas, cherry tomatoes, cucumber, red onion, and parsley.

In a small bowl, whisk together the tahini, lemon juice, water, olive oil, minced garlic, salt, and pepper to create the dressing.

Pour the dressing over the salad and toss gently to coat the ingredients evenly.

Serve immediately or refrigerate until ready to eat. This refreshing salad is a great way to incorporate anti-inflammatory ingredients.

Nutritional Value (per serving):

Calories: 350

Protein: 12g

Carbohydrates: 32g

Fiber: 9g

Fat: 20g

Saturated Fat: 2g

Sodium: 320mg

Cooking Time: 15 minutes

30. Roasted Vegetable and Quinoa Buddha Bowl

Ingredients:

1 cup quinoa, rinsed

2 cups water or vegetable broth

1 sweet potato, peeled and diced

1 zucchini, sliced

1 red bell pepper, sliced

1 cup cherry tomatoes, halved

1 tablespoon of olive oil

1 teaspoon smoked paprika

1 teaspoon of cumin

Salt and pepper to taste

2 cups mixed greens (e.g., kale, arugula, spinach)

1/4 cup hummus

Lemon wedges for garnish (optional)

Preparation Method:

Preheat the oven to 400°F (200°C).

In a saucepan, combine quinoa and water or vegetable broth. Bring to a boil, then reduce heat to low, cover, and simmer for 15-20 minutes or until quinoa is cooked.

On a baking sheet, toss sweet potato, zucchini, red bell pepper, and cherry tomatoes with olive oil, smoked paprika, cumin, salt, and pepper. Roast in the preheated oven for 20–25 minutes or until vegetables are tender and slightly caramelized.

Assemble the bowls by dividing the cooked quinoa among the serving bowls. Top with roasted vegetables and mixed greens.

Drizzle each bowl with hummus and garnish with lemon wedges if desired.

Nutritional Value (per serving):

Calories: 450

Protein: 14g

Carbohydrates: 75g

Fiber: 13g

Fat: 12g

Saturated Fat: 2g

Sodium: 320mg

Cooking time: 30 minutes

CONCLUSION

Finally, this Osteoarthritis Plant-Based Diet Cookbook for Beginners includes a variety of tasty and nutritious meals designed to promote joint health and general well-being. Each dish is made with carefully chosen plant-based components recognized for their anti-inflammatory effects, offering a tasty path to controlling osteoarthritis. From Quinoa and Vegetable Stuffed Bell Peppers to Sweet Potato and Black Bean Chili, these dishes are not only simple to prepare but also high in important nutrients that promote joint health and reduce inflammation.

Taking on this plant-based culinary expedition may be a transformative experience, encouraging a more holistic approach to health. By adding these dishes to your everyday routine, you are adopting a lifestyle that benefits your joints and feeds your body. The brilliant colors, diversified tastes, and nutrient-dense foods in these dishes make switching to a plant-based diet both pleasurable and sustainable.

As you begin on this path, keep in mind that each step toward a healthy life is one step closer to a more vibrant, pain-free future. Accept the nourishing power of plant-based nutrition and let this cookbook take you on a joyful and gratifying road to controlling osteoarthritis. Your health is an investment, and choosing these plant-based treats means investing in a brighter, more vibrant future. Your body deserves the finest, so let plant-based nutrition be the key to achieving maximum health.

Thank you for exploring the Osteoarthritis Plant-Based Diet Cookbook for Beginners! Your commitment to health is inspiring. We hope these recipes bring joy to your kitchen and vitality to your life. May your journey be filled with delicious moments and the nourishment your body truly deserves. Cheers to a vibrant you!

Printed in Great Britain
by Amazon